ONE BUGGING BBB BEEP

A Musical Memoir

ONE BUGGING BBB BEEP
Copyright © 2014, Zach Roberts

All Rights Reserved

One Bugging BBB Beep
A Musical Memoir

The Complete Book and Lyrics

As Written and Performed by
Zach Roberts

Lyrics by
Sir Elton John
Lynn Ahrens
Stephen Flaherty
Stephen Trask
Lionel Richie
Jason Robert Brown
Nic Cester
Tom Kitt
Brian Yorkey
James Blunt

Contents

A Note from the Author

I had been sitting in the 12th row of the Gerald Schoenfeld theatre in New York City the first time I saw the Jason Robert Brown, Marsha Norman masterpiece that was *The Bridges of Madison County.* I was sobbing hysterically because I had never seen or heard something so beautiful in my life. I had just had my heart broken by a scumbag and I felt as if Mr. Brown had captured that feeling and put it on stage in his gorgeous score. I had never read *The Bridges of Madison County* by Robert James Waller, nor had I seen the Meryl Streep / Clint Eastwood film adaptation, so I didn't know the story well enough to prepare myself for the emotionally heart wrenching story I was seeing play out in front of me. The chemistry between Steven Pasquale and Kelli O'Hara (the original cast of this splendid production) has haunted my memory to this very day. I left the theatre a hot mess of tears with a renewed focus on musical theatre. I knew that I wanted to perform in a show like *Bridges;* I knew had to pursue this for the rest of my life.

It was with that same emotional, cathartic experience that I sat down to write my own show, *One Bugging BBB Beep.* I knew that I wanted the story to focus on my own heartbreak and pain. I knew that I wanted the story to elicit a strong emotional response and I knew that I wanted to include songs that helped garner that response.

It is with great pride that I present, in its entirety, my show, *One Bugging BBB Beep,* that you may someday read it and remember fondly your first love, your first heartbreak, your first loss, and find solace in the simple fact that you are not alone in your pain.

With Love,
Zach Roberts

Production Note

One Bugging BBB Beep
Book by Zach Roberts
Music and Lyrics by Various Artists
Directed by Rachel Jensen, Vicki Perks, Zach Roberts

One Bugging BBB Beep was originally produced at the
Northwestern Junior / Senior High School Cafetorium by
Zach Roberts. It opened on May 2, 2015 to a sold-out
audience

In December of 2015, *One Bugging BBB Beep* won the 2015
Patsy Award for Outstanding Musical.

In April of 2016, Zach Roberts was awarded the 2016 Azooie
Award for Best Nonfiction Performance for his work in *One
Bugging BBB Beep.*

Cast and Credits

Cast

ZACH

Zach Roberts

Keyboard

Rachel Jensen

Musical Numbers

1. Don't Let the Sun Go Down on Me
2. Larger Than Life
3. The Origin of Love
4. Hello
5. Wondering
6. Wicked Little Town
7. Look What You've Done
8. You Don't Need to Love Me
9. Goodbye My Lover
10. It All Fades Away

Spoken lines are indicated in upper- and lowercase.

One Bugging BBB Beep
A Musical Memoir

Act 1

ZACH

(while curtain is closed, or blackout) Ladies and gentlemen! Welcome to this performance! I'm sure you're all looking at your Playbills, but if you're not, look at your Playbills. The first thing you'll notice is that the cover is a naked alien, the second thing you'll notice is that the title is *One Bugging BBB Beep*—you can thank Siri for that, that's all I'll say, moving on... This performance will be presented with one-count 'em- 1 five – count 'em- 1-2-3-4-five minute intermission. If you have to pee, do it then. If you would like to use your phone to take pictures, please do! If I see you texting, or having a phone call, I will Patti LuPone the show *(in Patti LuPone shouting voice)* WHO DO YOU THINK YOU ARE?! YOU HEARD THE ANNOUNCEMENT BEFORE THE SHOW! *(back to normal)* I'll do it! Mid-song! I don't care! Now without further ado, *One Bugging BBB Beep!*

1. Don't Let the Sun Go Down On Me

(curtain opens during first measure of song; onstage are two beds, one on stage right made with sheets and pillows, one on stage left--barren. There is a desk downstage that is empty. The set should be minimal as to keep the audience attention on the story, but upstage windows are optional and an upstage desk for the roommate as well)

ZACH
I CAN'T LIGHT NO MORE OF YOUR DARKNESS
ALL MY PICTURES
SEEM TO FADE TO
BLACK AND WHITE
I'M GROWING TIRED
AND TIME STANDS STILL BEFORE ME
FROZEN HERE ON THE LADDER OF MY LIFE

ZACH

TOO LATE TO SAVE MYSELF FROM FALLING,
I TOOK A CHANCE
AND CHANGED YOUR WAY OF LIFE!
BUT YOU MISREAD MY MEANING WHEN I MET YOU
CLOSED THE DOOR AND LEFT ME BLINDED
BY THE LIGHT!

DON'T LET THE SUN GO DOWN ON ME!
ALTHOUGH I SEARCH MYSELF,
IT'S ALWAYS SOMEONE ELSE I SEE...
I'D JUST ALLOW A FRAGMENT OF YOUR LIFE
TO WANDER FREE,
BUT LOSING EVERYTHING
IS LIKE THE SUN GOING DOWN ON ME!

I CAN'T FIND THE RIGHT ROMANTIC LINE!
BUT SEE ME ONCE AND SEE THE WAY I FEEL...
DON'T DISCARD ME
JUST BECAUSE YOU THINK I MEAN YOU HARM!
BUT THESE CUTS I HAVE,
OH, THEY NEED LOVE TO HELP THEM HEAL!

DON'T LET THE SUN GO DOWN ON ME
ALTHOUGH I SEARCH MYSELF,
IT'S ALWAYS SOMEONE ELSE I SEE...
I'D JUST ALLOW A FRAGMENT OF YOUR LIFE
TO WANDER FREE,
BUT LOSING EVERYTHING
IS LIKE THE SUN GOING DOWN ME!

ZACH

Our story tonight begins at Northwestern High School. Not this Northwestern Junior / Senior High School, but the Northwestern High School that is now torn down and is a grass lot. It was 2009, I was 14, and I had been looking for a hobby, for a while.

ZACH

I did karate for a minute, but it wasn't worth it—too much physical activity for me. I mean, they wanted me to run a five-minute mile to get a black belt? No.

The next thing that I tried, and I wish I were making this up, was to play the bagpipes. Seriously, my dad had a friend who played the bagpipes and he was like "I'll teach you how to play the bagpipes young man" and I did it. I played it once, put it down, and never touched it again because it was extremely weird.

For years I thought that performing was what I was meant to do. I had made hundreds of YouTube videos – most of which had to be taken down because they were "inappropriate for my age"—but that was something that I thought I would like to do. Stand in front of people and entertain them, hopefully. In seventh grade, Mrs. Jensen asked us why we chose choir over band and my answer was simple: to train my voice for the High School musicals—and she remembered that!

When she announced the musical, *My Favorite Year,* I didn't know what it was and I'm sure nobody else did either, but it turned out to be a great show! It's about Benjy Stone who is the youngest, newest writer on the biggest show in the 50s, *The King Kaiser Comedy Cavalcade,* which is essentially *Saturday Night Live,* and the week that the musical showcases is the biggest week of Benjy's life. His hero and the man he idolizes as his father, Alan Swann, is going to be the guest on the show and Benjy gets to look after him and show him around the city and get him to rehearsals and such, so he's poopin' he's so excited.

So, I went in and I auditioned. I'm not sure whether I had even hit puberty at the time, but I sang "Ain't No Sunshine" right to Mrs. Jensen. And when she posted the cast list I was surprised to see "Benjy Stone..........Zachary Roberts" ARE YOU KIDDING ME?! This is my first ever musical, my first audition, and I got the lead?? I was going to be Benjy Stone!

2. Larger Than Life

ZACH

UNCLE MORTY USED TO SEND ME TO THE MOVIES,
"HERE'S A NICKEL KID, CHEER UP AND GO!"
AND THOUGH I WAS ONLY SEVEN,
I DISCOVERED HEAVEN AT THE R.K.O.!

BLUE LIGHTS, PINK LIGHTS, STARS IN THE CEILING,
AN ORGAN AS BIG AS A BUICK, AND A SCREEN
AS TALL AS THE GREAT WALL OF CHINA!
RED RUGS, GOLD STAIRS, PORCELAIN ANGELS!
AND EVERYTHING BIGGER, AND BETTER, AND
LARGER THAN LIFE!

At first, I was strictly a Western man.... But then, one
Saturday afternoon, I saw *Defender of the Crown;* Warner
Brothers, 1941, Technicolor, starring.... Alan Swann!

DARING, LOYAL, KIND BUT COURAGEOUS,
A HERO AS BIG AS A BUICK, WITH A CAPE,
A SWORD, AND A BEVVY OF MAIDENS,
HE WAS MOVIES, ME? I WAS SEVEN.
AND GEE, HE WAS BIGGER, AND BETTER, AND
LARGER THAN LIFE!

SEE, LIFE WASN'T CAPES
AND FLASHING SWORDS AND PARAPETS.
LIFE WASN'T ALAN SWANN OR ROBIN HOOD...
LIFE WAS YOUR FATHER GOING OUT
FOR CIGARETTES,
AND DECIDING HE WAS GOING OUT FOR GOOD...

"HERE'S A NICKEL KID, CHEER UP AND GO,
SWANN IS PLAYING AT THE R.K.O.!"

ZACH

Well, sure, it was possible! If he'd met my mom in '34, maybe had a fling with her in his cabana at the Chateau Marmot, well there was every reason to believe that there could be the remote possibility that the man who went out for the Chesterfields wasn't my real father at all! I wasn't some stupid kid whose father got tired of him and walked out. I was the bastard son of Alan Swann!

DARING, LOYAL, KIND BUT COURAGEOUS!
A HERO AS BIG AS I NEEDED
IN THE TECHNICOLOR EMBRACE OF A MAIDEN!
SWANN MY HERO AND POSSIBLE FATHER...
HE STOOD, AND HE FOUGHT, AND HE NEVER RAN,
OH NO... HE WAS BIGGER, AND BETTER, AND
LARGER THAN LIFE!
AND HE LIVED FOR ME AT THE R.K.O.!

ZACH

Being in *My Favorite Year* was easily one of the greatest experiences of my life. I made some of the best friendships I've ever had and I learned so much about performing and theatre etiquette in general. For example, if your show is scheduled to start at 7:00, you're still on time if you start before 7:07, anything after that and you're late, but maybe that was just an old wives tale. I learned a lot, but the biggest thing that I realized was—this is it. This is what I was meant to do with the rest of my life. I had found my "other half" if you will.

See, in our society, we talk a lot about our need to find another person to complete us. We tell ourselves that we're some sort of "half-monster" until we find the person that "completes us." And it's a beautiful sentiment, but why couldn't I just perform for the rest of my life and have thirteen cats? We all tell ourselves that one day he'll come and he'll rush us off our feet and we'll ride into the sunset on a white horse and live happily ever after.

ZACH

Well, that didn't happen for me. I always thought that in High School I would meet the man of my dreams and we would live happily and we would tell our children of all of our romantic escapades from high school till death.... That didn't happen. So, I thought, maybe college! But I was all right with waiting. I was happy performing every opportunity I had, which turned out to be ten musicals with Northwestern.

What I learned from that was, I was all right doing this—I was fine, this was my other half. I loved performing. But... That didn't mean I wasn't looking...

2. The Origin of Love

ZACH

WHEN THE EARTH WAS STILL FLAT
AND CLOUDS MADE OF FIRE, MOUNTAINS
STRETCHED UP TO THE SKY, SOMETIMES HIGHER.
FOLKS ROAMED THE EARTH LIKE
BIG ROLLING KEGS THEY HAD TWO SETS OF ARMS,
THEY HAD TWO SETS OF LEGS, THEY HAD
TWO FACES PEERING OUT OF ONE GIANT HEAD
SO THEY COULD WATCH ALL AROUND THEM AS
THEY TALKED WHILE THEY READ AND THEY
NEVER KNEW NOTHING OF LOVE, IT WAS BEFORE
THE ORIGIN OF LOVE

AND THERE WERE THREE SEXES THEN, ONE THAT
LOOKED LIKE TWO MEN GLUED UP BACK TO BACK
CALLED 'THE CHILDREN OF THE SUN' AND
SIMILAR IN SHAPE AND GIRTH WERE 'THE
CHILDREN OF THE EARTH' THEY LOOKED LIKE
TWO GIRLS ROLLED UP IN ONE... AND 'THE
CHILDREN OF THE MOON' LOOKED LIKE A FORK
SHOVED ON A SPOON, THEY WERE PART SUN, PART
EARTH, PART DAUGHTER, PART SON...
OOO, THE ORIGIN OF LOVE...

ZACH

NOW THE GODS GREW QUITE SCARED OF OUR
STRENGTH AND DEFIANCE AND THOR SAID 'I'M
GONNA KILL 'EM ALL WITH MY HAMMER, LIKE I
KILLED THE GIANTS,' BUT ZEUS SAID, 'NO, YOU'D
BETTER LET ME USE MY LIGHTNING LIKE
SCISSORS LIKE I CUT THE LEGS OFF THE WHALES,
DINOSAURS INTO LIZARDS,' AND THEN HE
GRABBED UP SOME BOLTS, HE LET OUT A LAUGH,
SAID, 'I'LL SPLIT THEM RIGHT DOWN THE MIDDLE,
GONNA CUT 'EM RIGHT UP IN HALF,' AND THE
STORM CLOUDS GATHERED ABOVE INTO GREAT
BALLS OF FIRE!

AND THEN FIRE SHOT DOWN FROM THE SKY IN
BOLTS LIKE SHINING BLADES OF A KNIFE! AND IT
RIPPED RIGHT THROUGH THE FLESH OF THE
CHILDREN OF THE SUN AND THE MOON AND THE
EARTH! AND SOME INDIAN GOD SEWED THE
WOUND UP TO A HOLE, PULLED IT ROUND TO OUR
BELLY TO REMIND US THE PRICE WE PAID! AND
OSIRIS, THE GODS OF THE NILE, GATHERED UP A
BIG STORM TO BLOW A HURRICANE TO SCATTER
US AWAY IN A FLOOD OF WIND AND RAIN, A SEA
OF TIDAL WAVES TO WASH US ALL AWAY! IF WE
DON'T BEHAVE, THEY'LL CUT US DOWN AGAIN!
WE'LL BE HOPPIN' ROUND ON ONE FOOT, AND
LOOKIN' THROUGH ONE EYE!

THE LAST TIME I SAW YOU, WE'D JUST SPLIT IN
TWO, YOU WERE LOOKIN' AT ME, I WAS LOOKIN'
AT YOU. YOU HAD A WAY SO FAMILIAR I COULD
NOT RECOGNIZE CUZ YOU HAD BLOOD ON YOUR
FACE, I HAD BLOOD IN MY EYES BUT I COULD
SWEAR BY YOUR EXPRESSION THAT THE PAIN
DOWN IN YOUR SOUL WAS THE SAME AS THE ONE
DOWN IN MINE!

ZACH

OH, THAT'S THE PAIN THAT CUTS A STRAIGHT LINE DOWN THROUGH THE HEART! WE CALL IT LOVE! WE WRAPPED OUR ARMS AROUND EACH OTHER, TRY AND SHOVE OURSELVES BACK TOGETHER, WE WERE MAKING LOVE... MAKING LOVE.

IT WAS A COLD, DARK EVENING SUCH A LONG TIME AGO WHEN BY THE MIGHTY HAND OF JOB, IT WAS A SAD STORY HOW WE BECAME LONELY TWO LEGGED CREATURES; IT'S THE STORY OF THE ORIGIN OF LOVE, THAT'S THE ORIGIN OF LOVE!

ZACH

Because of this whole "other half" thing we tell ourselves, I think that somewhere, deep down, I always thought I would fall in love in college. So, when Mrs. Rutan suggested Columbia College Chicago, I think that love was in the back of my mind. It didn't factor into my decision, but there was definitely a little voice in the back of my head saying, "hey, buddy! You might fall in love," but I didn't really listen to it! I picked the school because I thought they had a great performing arts program. I thought this is what I want to do for the rest of my life, so why go to school and study law as a backup plan, when I could go to school and study what I love and live happily ever after? So I picked Columbia and when it was time to move in, I had already sent my roommates an email. I had three roommates, because we had a full apartment. We had two bedrooms, a kitchen, a bathroom and a living room all to ourselves. In one bedroom we had Daniel from Saint Paul, Minnesota and Josh from Atlanta, Georgia. The other room was for Zach from Decatur, Illinois and myself.

You can imagine as I sent this email it was kind of awkward, as it was bound to be.

ZACH

I was preparing to move in with three random people I'd never met before in my entire life! I sent out my email saying, "hello, I'm Zach, I'm a performing arts major, I'm excited to move in, hope you don't kill me." The only person to ever respond to that email was Zach. He told me he was a Fashion Photography major, that he was from Decatur, Illinois and that he had just graduated valedictorian of his class.

He seemed like a nice guy and we started texting a lot. Over the course of a few weeks, we had become sort of friendly with one another by the time move-in came. We show up there that day and there's this very handsome young man coming to the door to greet us. "Hello!" he says. He comes up and shakes my hand and he has the softest hands I've ever felt. The only hands softer are Barack Hussein Obama's—and I should know, because I met him *(hair toss)*.

I noticed he had wonderful hair... and eyes... and his smile was nice, he had little dimples, his teeth were pearly white, he was dressed nicely and.... he had nice features, I was pleased. It's always nice to have one attractive roommate, because let's talk about the other two for a second. Daniel—long, ratty hair who never showered, and Josh—the clean freak who cleaned literally everyday and then moved out because the apartment was too gross, but that's a whole different musical.

As Zach and I unpacked our stuff in our room, it felt like we were already friends. I could tell it wasn't going to be too much longer before I started to fall for him...

4. Hello

(periodically throughout the song, ZACH should unpack a box of assorted items to move in and decorate the apartment. Items included in the original production were a framed photo of ZACH and Vice President Joseph Biden, a Hillary Clinton bobble head, an Obama themed Root Beer in addition to notebooks, pens, pencils and textbooks)

ZACH

I'VE BEEN ALONE WITH YOU INSIDE MY MIND
AND IN MY DREAMS I'VE KISSED YOUR LIPS
A THOUSAND TIMES, I SOMETIMES SEE YOU
PASS OUTSIDE MY DOOR

HELLO, IS IT ME YOU'RE LOOKING FOR?
I CAN SEE IT IN YOUR EYES
I CAN SEE IT IN YOUR SMILE,
YOU'RE ALL I'VE EVER WANTED AND
MY ARMS ARE OPEN WIDE!
CAUSE YOU KNOW JUST WHAT TO SAY,
AND YOU KNOW JUST WHAT TO DO
AND I WANT TO TELL YOU SO MUCH I LOVE YOU.

I LONG TO SEE THE SUNLIGHT IN YOUR HAIR
AND TELL YOU TIME AND TIME AGAIN
HOW MUCH I CARE. SOMETIMES I FEEL
MY HEART WILL OVERFLOW!

HELLO! IS IT ME YOU'RE LOOKING FOR?
CUZ I WONDER WHERE YOU ARE
AND I WONDER WHAT YOU DO
ARE YOU SOMEWHERE FEELING LONELY?
OR IS SOMEONE LOVING YOU?
TELL ME HOW TO WIN YOUR HEART,
FOR I HAVEN'T GOT A CLUE...
BUT LET ME START BY SAYING, I LOVE YOU.

HELLO! I'VE JUST GOT TO LET YOU KNOW!
CUZ I WONDER WHERE YOU ARE!
AND I WONDER WHAT YOU DO!
ARE YOU SOMEWHERE FEELING LONELY?
OR IS SOMEONE LOVING YOU?
TELL ME HOW TO WIN YOUR HEART!
FOR I HAVEN'T GOT A CLUE!
BUT LET ME START BY SAYING... I LOVE YOU...

ZACH

Over the next couple of days, Zach and I started hanging out a lot. For me, it was partly necessity, because I didn't know a single living soul in Chicago except for Oprah Winfrey. The only person I really had to hang out with was Zach... Don't get me wrong...I enjoyed it. You know when you meet someone whether you're going to be friends the rest of your life or if you're going to hate them forever... Well, I thought friends at first.

We just hit it off! We did everything together. We went to see the abandoned Harpo Studios and I was so excited, I looked like a crazy person circling the building screaming at the random memories of *The Oprah Winfrey Show*. But, it was when I caught him looking at me in the reflection of the subway windows, or how he sat so close to me sometimes... But it wasn't until I met the girls across the hall that I thought maybe there was something more than friendship between the two of us.

You see we had to attend a floor meeting where you all sit in a circle and you rip off pieces of toilet paper from the roll and "for each piece of toilet paper you have to say a fact about yourself." It's stupid. It's always the worst part of getting to know your classmates. It's like that stupid word association "name something that starts with the same letter as your name!" and mine is always Zucchini Zach, or "name your favorite animal that shares your letter," and it's Zebra Zach and it's just the absolute worst. At this meeting, I met the four girls who would become my best friends. They invited me over to dance to ABBA with them and as a flaming homosexual I couldn't turn down a chance to belt "Dancing Queen." We had a great time. We shared secrets that some people still don't know. We had a lot in common— there was Josey and Becca from Illinois and Tori and Jules from Florida. The first thing they asked after we dated our baby boi hearts out was "are you dating that boy?" HAHAHA, no. In a perfect world, but no.

ZACH

See, I didn't know, it's hard, because you can't just walk up to someone and ask them "ya like boys?" If they're conservative they're going to be like "ABSOLUTELY NOT, HOW DARE YOU?! I HAVE A GIRLFRIEND AT HOME," and you just can't do it! It's too awkward! Hence, the plight of the LGBT community. But, they convinced me to do it. So, I barge into his room while he's doing homework and I ease into it. "Hey, bud, how are you, how's your day?" and he says "Oh, good, how's yours?" "Oh, it's great, ya gay?" He laughs "Oh, no, no, no, I'm not looking for a relationship, sorry to disappoint. Byeeeee" and he leaves. Are you kidding me? You're "not looking for a relationship?" You're nineteen! You're looking for a relationship, okay!?

That's a cop-out! It was the same thing I would've said if you'd asked me in seventh grade. "No way, man, I'm not gay, I like boobs and stuff." It was the 19-year-old version of that. "I've gotta focus on my studies." Maybe I should've listened to him. But I kept telling myself that it had to be a cop-out, that he was so deep in the closet... COME OUT, COME OUT WHEREVER YOU ARE! Because, I just kept thinking there's something special here.... What if we're meant to be? What if this is who I'm going to spend the rest of my life with? What if he's straight? What if he hates me? What if he likes me? What if he's... the one?

5. Wondering

ZACH

(during this song, ZACH is packing his backpack to go to class)
A LITTLE TWINGE,
A LITTLE SHOCK,
A LITTLE WHISPER AT
THE BOTTOM OF YOUR MEMORY,
A SUDDEN WIND,
A GENTLE KNOCK AND THEN

ZACH

A RUSTLE IN THE LEAVES...
YOU HOLD YOUR BREATH, YOU CHECK THE LOCK,
YOU REASSURE YOURSELF THERE'S NOTHING AT
THE WINDOW...

BUT YOU'RE WONDERING,
YOU'RE WONDERING,
YOU'RE WONDERING WHAT THAT WAS...
NOTHING'S GONNA HAPPEN,
NOTHING'S GONNA HAPPEN...

YOU TURN A KEY,
YOU FLIP A SWITCH,
YOU SETTLE BACK INTO THE BLISSFUL
UNFAMILIAR, YOU CLOSE YOUR EYES
BUT THERE'S AN ITCH,
A LITTLE HURT YOUR HEART RETREIVES,
BUT YOU IGNORE THE TINY TWITCH,
PRETEND THE FEELING WILL BE GONE
BEFORE THE MORNING...

BUT YOU'RE WONDERING,
YOU'RE WONDERING,
YOU'RE WONDERING WHERE YOU ARE...
NOTHING'S GONNA HAPPEN,
NOTHING'S GONNA HAPPEN...

BUT WOULDN'T IT BE FINE TO SHARE
THE WEATHER IN HER EYES, HER HAIR,
HER FOOTSTEPS AS SHE CLIMBS THE STAIR,
THE SHADOW IN HER LIGHT?
BUT EVERYTHING YOU KNOW IS TRUE,
AND EVERYTHING YOU WANT TO DO,
AND EVERYTHING THAT MAKES YOU YOU
COLLIDES AGAINST THE NIGHT...
AND NOTHING'S BLACK AND WHITE....

ZACH
BUT YOU'RE WONDERING,
YOU'RE WONDERING,
YOU'RE WONDERING WHAT TO DO,
YOU'RE WONDERING,
YOU'RE WONDERING,
YOU'RE WONDERING IF IT'S TRUE...
NOTHING'S GONNA HAPPEN...
NOTHING HAS TO HAPPEN...

(ZACH gathers his things and puts on his backpack. HE heads out stage right and turns back to look longingly at the other Zach's bed before turning and leaving for class.)

(BLACKOUT)

(CURTAIN)

(END ACT 1)

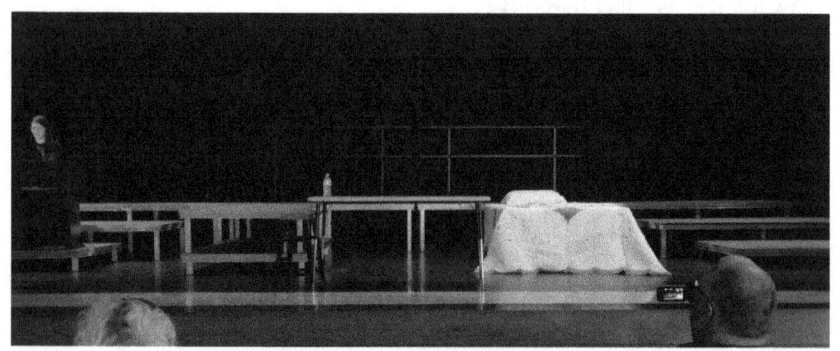

(Top: Set Design for *One Bugging BBB Beep* Act One)

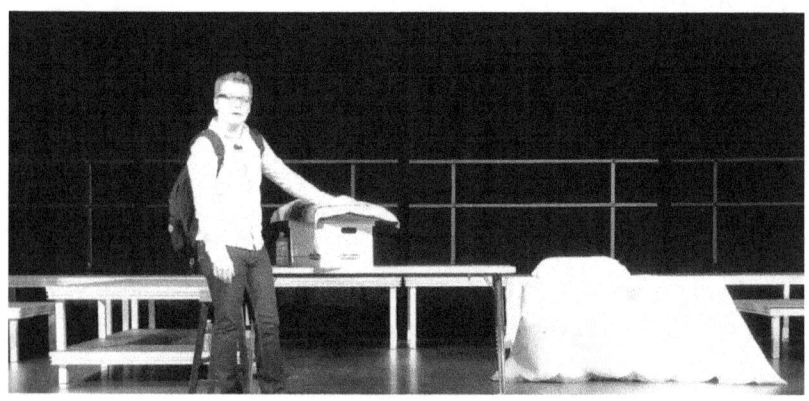

(Bottom: Zach moves to Chicago)

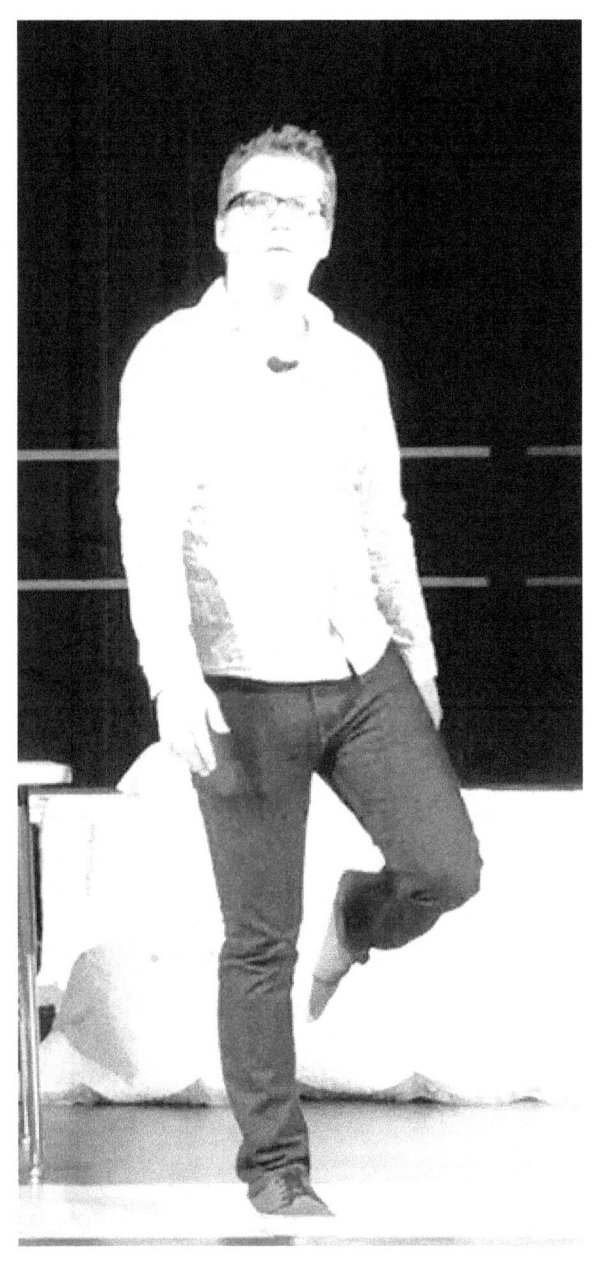

(Zach Roberts performs "The Origin of Love")

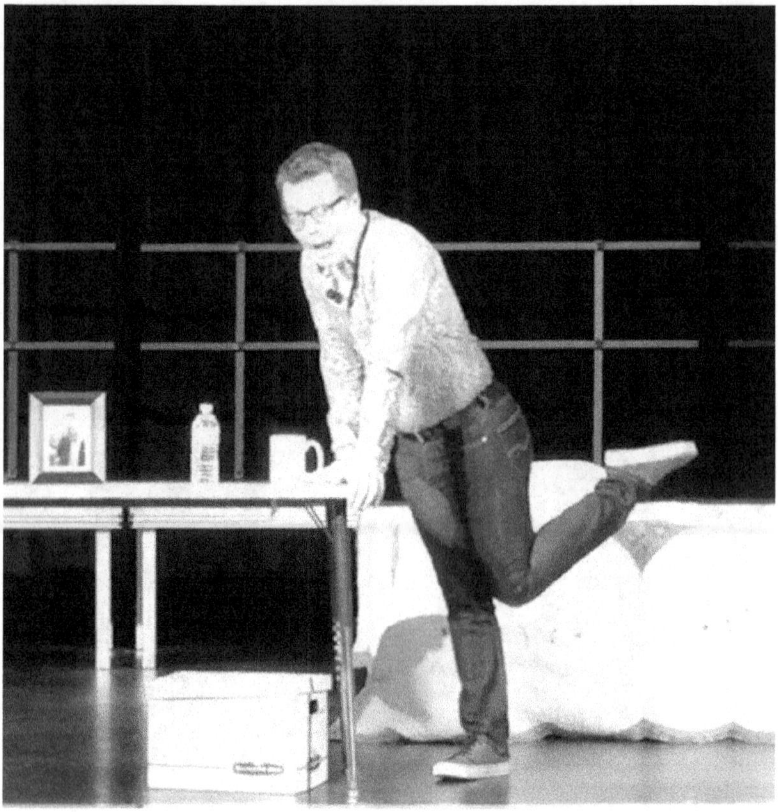

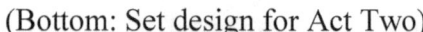

(Top: "Are we gonna kiss? Are we gonna kiss?")

(Bottom: Set design for Act Two)

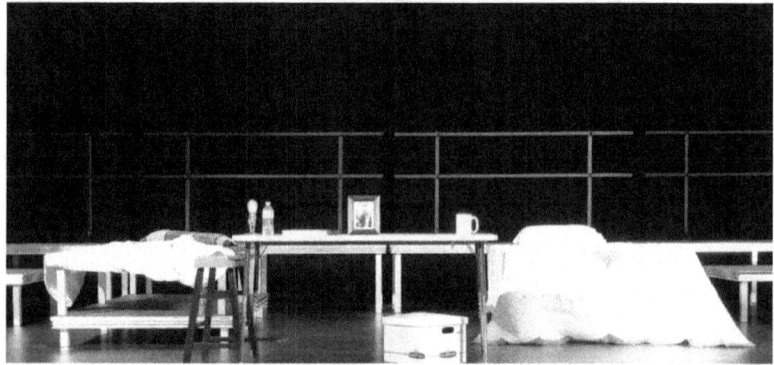

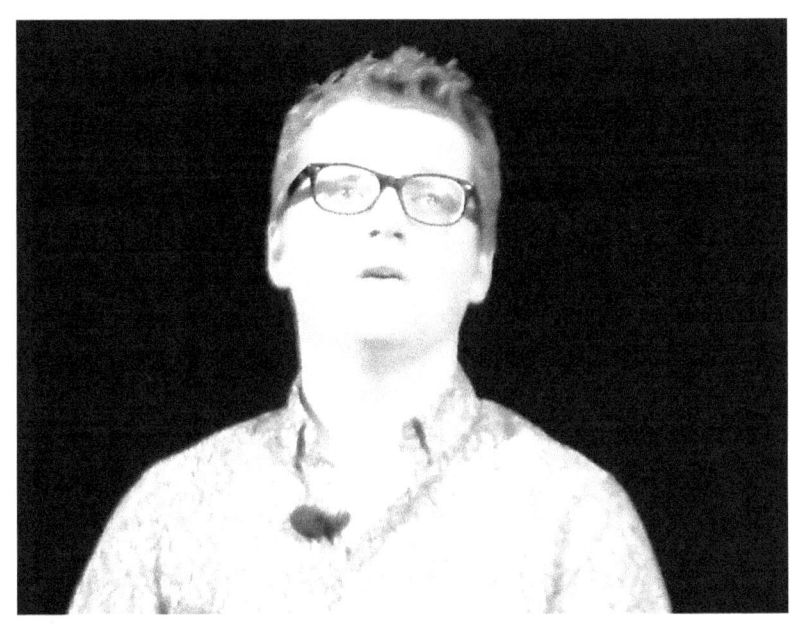

(Top: "Why is he doing this?")

(Bottom: Zach Roberts performs "Goodbye My Lover")

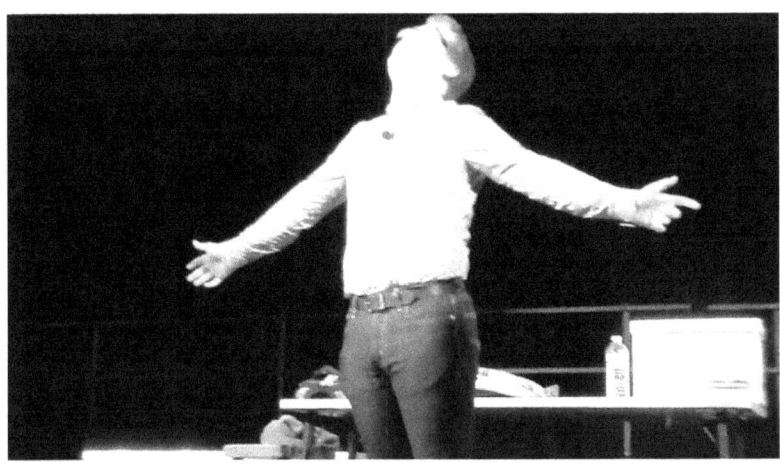

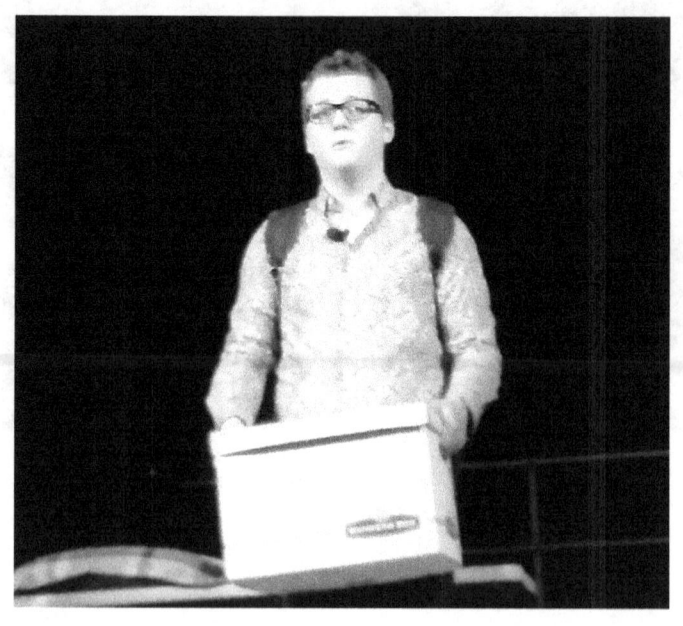

("It all fades away... But you...)

Act 2

ZACH

(the curtain opens to the dorm room empty of life, but full of random and unnecessary knick-knacks from Act 1. After a beat, ZACH enters from stage right, when centered...) Over the next couple of months, Zach and I got a lot closer than I really ever thought we would. We did literally everything together. We went shopping, watched *America's Next Top Model* together... We would just be together always. We would lie in our separate beds and talk about life until two or three in the morning—or until one of us passed out because we had classes to attend. We were thick as thieves as they say...we stole everything.

He was, without a doubt, my best friend at that time. The girls across the hall were some of the funniest people I had ever met. We were so close that, well, we were never apart. I mean, we lived *feet* apart and we would text each other when we would go our separate ways for the night and say, "omigosh I miss you so much!" We were your basic High School teenagers.

I really enjoyed spending time with all of them, but specifically Zach. One time in particular, my family came up to surprise me with a visit. I swear to you, I knew nothing about it and was completely oblivious the entire time. They texted Zach and told him that they were going to come visit. He played along. He told me we needed to clean the apartment because *his* parents were coming, and thank goodness he did, because it wasn't clean AT ALL and I would've been entirely embarrassed if my parents came into our place and there was an entire garbage can overflowing with Coke cans... Actually, I probably would've been proud....

Anyway, I went downstairs on the day that his parents were supposed to arrive. I opened the door expecting people who were not my family and there they all are holding a sign and yelling "SURPRISE!"

ZACH

I was SO happy, I hadn't seen them in two months and up until this point I hadn't gone 48 hours without seeing or talking to them in person. But, I was having such a great time in Chicago, that I hadn't really noticed that I missed them. So, they show up and I'm like "oh, I'm so happy you're here but I have absolutely no idea what to do with you!"

That night, my sister ended up staying with us in our extra bed—Josh had moved out by this point, because the apartment was *(in Josh voice)* "a pig-sty, Zach, and I am not livin' here anymo' goodbye," *(regular voice)*.... See ya! Good riddance... *(clarifying to audience)* He smelled like baby-powder. He moved out and we had an empty bed, so I let my sister stay with us. We had a lot of fun, we snuck her back and forth across the hall because you're not supposed to have overnight visitors under the age of 18 apparently—go to college, you'll learn a lot about the stupid rules and guidelines of dorm-living.

We're in our apartment and we're dancing to ABBA in the windowsills, waving at passersby on the street, and throwing glow sticks down to hobos—just having a great time. It's actually one of the best times I can remember having in Chicago where everyone was there. There were so many times where someone would have to leave for class or go to sleep or study that this was the first and only time we ever all hung out simultaneously and I loved every second of it.

At one point in the evening, while everyone was distracted, Zach pulls me into our room and closes the door behind him. I immediately start thinking "are we gonna kiss? Are we gonna kiss?"

We didn't kiss, BUT, he looked me in the eyes and he smiled his beautiful smile and he says... "I love... spending time with you." Then he hugged me and left the room. I had to sit on my bed for a while because I was screaming at the top of my lungs.

ZACH

I was the happiest I can remember being at that time during that night.

But it wasn't just that. If I were to stand up here and tell you every adorable thing that happened, we would be here for a week. We would go to Target together, walk around Chicago while he took photos for his classes... He would come to some of my classes and watch the stupid stuff we were doing... We made sure we had dinner ready for each other whenever we got home from class—nothing fancy, but I do bake a splendid frozen chicken. It was wonderful.

But it was in the way he looked at me. Or in the way he talked about me to other people. Or the way he protected me when LIAM moved in—that's a whole other show.

It was in the way he talked about me when I wasn't around. It was in the way he let me put my head on his shoulder while we were watching *American Horror Story*. It was in the way he fed me a lima bean at Josey's grandparent's house. Or the way he would fix the collar on my jacket before I left—he'd brush the lint of my shoulders and hug me everyday. When we met new people he would introduce us as "we're Zach," –THAT'S ADORABLE, our celebrity couple name was 'Zach.'

But it was in all of those small moments when it was just the two of us—when we were at Bar Louie having a gorgeous candlelit dinner over burgers, fries and coke, where we talked about our dreams and hopes and desires, where we came from and where we were going. It was in those moments that I knew... When he laughs I am filled with an ancient clarity... He's the one. The one who was taken. But this time there's no blood on his face and no blood in my eyes. He's the one. I've never been more certain of anything in my life... He is the one.

6. Wicked Little Town

(ZACH performs this song seated on the other Zach's bed)

ZACH

YOU KNOW THE SUN IS IN YOUR EYES
AND HURRICANES AND RAINS
BLACK AND CLOUDY SKIES
YOU'RE RUNNING UP AND DOWN THAT HILL
YOU TURN IT ON AND OFF AT WILL
THERE'S NOTHING HERE TO THRILL OR BRING YOU
DOWN, AND IF YOU'VE GOT NO OTHER CHOICE,
YOU KNOW YOU CAN FOLLOW MY VOICE
THROUGH THE DARK TURNS AND NOISE OF THIS
WICKED LITTLE TOWN...

WELL, LADY LUCK HAS LED YOU HERE...
BUT THEY'RE SO TWISTED UP,
THEY'LL TWIST YOU UP I FEAR.
THE PIOUS, HATEFUL, AND DEVOUT,
YOU'RE TURNING TRICKS
TILL YOU'RE TURNED OUT
THE WIND SO COLD IT BURNS
YOU'RE BURNING OUT AND BLOWING ROUND
AND IF YOU'VE GOT NO OTHER CHOICE
YOU KNOW YOU CAN FOLLOW MY VOICE
THROUGH THE DARK TURNS AND NOISE OF THIS
WICKED LITTLE TOWN...

THE FATES ARE VICIOUS AND THEY'RE CRUEL...
YOU LEARN TOO LATE YOU'VE USED TWO WISHES
LIKE A FOOL...
AND THEN YOU'RE SOMEONE YOU ARE NOT
AND JUNCTION CITY AIN'T THE SPOT
REMEMBER MRS. LOTT AND
WHEN SHE TURNED AROUND...
AND IF YOU'VE GOT NO OTHER CHOICE
YOU KNOW YOU CAN FOLLOW MY VOICE
THROUGH THE DARK TURNS AND NOISE OF THIS
WICKED LITTLE TOWN...

ZACH

By the time finals week had arrived, things were noticeably different. Where we used to spend every waking moment together, it was suddenly every once in a while. That last week... he was so distant that I thought I had done something wrong. I'd have dinner ready when he came home and he said he'd already eaten. I had plans for the two of us; he said he already was doing something else.

The night before we left, he said he was going to the library to study for finals. He needed to get a good grade so he could keep his scholarship in order to return for the next semester, so I wasn't going to say no... I was sitting on my bed after he left, watching something on Netflix and I thought... Why am I sitting here being sad, why do I feel like I did something wrong, I know I didn't... So, I decided to go across the hall.

I figured I could go over there and hang out with my friends, have a good time and by the time Zach was done studying he could join us and everything would be okay again. I go over and knock on the door... and they don't answer... I know they're in there, I can hear their TV, I can hear them talking and moving around—the walls are paper-thin. I know they're home. Something was wrong... For the life of me, I didn't know what it was. Everything was going so well and now right before we leave it was all crashing down around me for no reason.

"Hey!" Becca pokes her head out of the door. She's always been the nicest of the group. She tells you exactly what's going on whether it's something you want to hear or not. "Sorry about that," she says, "Zach's over... and he doesn't want to see you..."

"Why not?"

She says... "I think he knows how you feel about him... and I think he doesn't feel the same... I don't know why he doesn't want to talk to you."

I started crying in the hallway. People were coming in and out of their apartments giving me strange looks.

ZACH

I'm having an emotional breakdown, sobbing into Becca's arms asking a bunch of questions, "how," "why," "why is he doing this," "why is this happening to me, everything was perfect..."

"I'll send him over to talk to you."

I sit on my bed and I start calling friends at home. I wanted someone to talk to—to tell me everything was going to be okay, that maybe he was going to tell me he loved me too. Or maybe just to tell me that I would get through it... Nobody answered. I really wanted to talk to someone...

He walks in the door and it's the first time there's ever been awkward tension between us. Not even when we moved in and didn't know each other did it feel like this. This is the first time I ever dreaded him walking through the door.

"We need to talk," he says.

"Yeah, I guess we do."

"Listen... I've known how you felt about me for awhile and I just... don't... feel the same way about you."

"Is it... Is it because you're straight?"

"No. I'm not straight; I just don't like you like that... You can't help who you're attracted to, I mean, I'm sure you didn't want to fall head-over-heels for me, but here we are."

Even as he was saying this, in my mind I thought there was still hope; he liked guys after all... So, I asked him. "I need to know and I need you to tell me in the simplest form whether there will ever be anything between us."

"...No. I'm sorry, but everything that you thought was special between us just meant nothing to me."

I could hear my heart break. I could feel the tears running down my cheek and I could see that he didn't care. He had done what he'd set out to do and now he was packing...

Even though he was the one breaking my heart, even though I knew I hadn't done anything wrong, the only thing I could think to say was... "I'm sorry."

---

7. Look What You've Done

(there is an uncomfortably long pause before this song begins. ZACH walks around the room, looking at the other Zach's bed, longing for the days when all was perfect between them)

ZACH

TAKE MY PHOTO OFF THE WALL
IF IT JUST WON'T SING FOR YOU.
CAUSE ALL THAT'S LEFT HAS GONE AWAY
AND THERE'S NOTHING THERE FOR YOU TO
PROVE.

OH, LOOK WHAT YOU'VE DONE
YOU'VE MADE A FOOL OF EVERYONE...
OH WELL, IT SEEMS LIKE SUCH FUN
UNTIL YOU LOSE WHAT YOU HAD WON.

GIVE ME BACK MY POINT OF VIEW
CAUSE I JUST WON'T THINK FOR YOU
I CAN HARDLY HEAR YOU SAY
"WHAT SHOULD I DO?"
WELL, YOU CHOOSE!

OH, LOOK WHAT YOU'VE DONE
YOU'VE MADE A FOOL OF EVERYONE!
OH WELL, IT SEEMS LIKE SUCH FUN
UNTIL YOU LOSE WHAT YOU HAD WON.
OH, LOOK WHAT YOU'VE DONE
YOU'VE MADE A FOOL OF EVERYONE.
A FOOL OF EVERYONE.
A FOOL OF EVERYONE!
TAKE MY PHOTO OFF THE WALL
IF IT JUST WON'T SING FOR YOU...
CAUSE ALL THAT'S LEFT HAS GONE AWAY
AND THERE'S NOTHING THERE FOR YOU TO DO...

ZACH

OH, LOOK WHAT YOU'VE DONE
YOU'VE MADE A FOOL OF EVERYONE!
OH WELL, IT SEEMS LIKE SUCH FUN
UNTIL YOU LOSE WHAT YOU HAD WON.
OH, LOOK WHAT YOU'VE DONE
YOU'VE MADE A FOOL EVERYONE!
A FOOL OF EVERYONE!
A FOOL OF EVERYONE!

ZACH

The last thing he said to me at Union Station before he got on his train home was "this doesn't have to change anything between us. I don't want it to be awkward when we get back, we can still be friends. I'm not going to stop talking to you because of this. Just know that going forward it's a different relationship."

I would've rather had him in my life as a friend than not at all. So, I went home. I cried on the train. I got off and saw my mom waiting for me and cried. I got home and I lay in bed and I cried. I had never felt a pain like that before. Every time I went out with my friends all I wanted to talk about was Zach and Josey and Jules and why do they hate me and why am I so ugly and what did I do? Because clearly I must've done something.

It got to the point where every time dinner was over, my mom would be doing dishes and turn around and ask me if I was okay... I couldn't even say no because I was already in tears. But I worked hard! I thought if I got all of the pain and tears out of the way that by the time I got back everything would be peachy keen and we would be the best of friends again—everything would go back to normal. We didn't talk much over Christmas break, other than holiday greetings. I decided I would go back to Chicago a week early so we could all hang out without having to go to class.

ZACH

Something in the back of my head told me, however, that nothing was going to be the same when I got back to Chicago.

I think every failed relationship ends with "lets stay friends"—but it never works out—and I thought for sure this was going to be one of those situations.

I saw the Chicago skyline come over the horizon and I was filled with dread to see the people that used to make me happy. I walked into our room and he was asleep. It was three in the afternoon; I unpacked my bag and lay in bed. I was waiting for him to wake up.

He finally woke up, we made small talk about my train ride and I said, "now that we're back, why don't we go to Bar Louie?" Seemed fitting to me, we went there every week, we were still friends supposedly, so let's go to a place where everybody knows our names.

"I've got a haircut, but maybe after. It's at five... Yeah, definitely after, text Josey and invite her!" Sweet! I immediately called my grandma and told her how wrong I had been, everything was great, he was right! He didn't lie—nothing is different! I could find the love of my life elsewhere, but I still had him as a friend! Everything was great, Mammaw, I was so dumb to think it was going to be different when I got back!

I took a shower, I got dressed, and I waited in the living room. And I waited. And I waited. And I waited. And I waited... And I waited... And I waited... And I waited... And... I waited... And I waited... Finally I went to bed.

He didn't come home until three in the morning and he didn't text me at all throughout the night to tell me he was all right or to reschedule. Josey wouldn't answer my texts, or my calls, or my knocks... I was right. Things were different.

The next day, he told me he and Josey were going to go to her grandparent's house and that I was going to have the apartment to myself. "I think you'll enjoy it, it's kind of nice having it to yourself," he said.

ZACH

No... I'm not going to enjoy that! I came back a week early to hang out with you and show you that everything could still be okay, but yes, go! Have a great time!

I blared Celine Dion so loud that if my neighbors had been home they would've been able to sing along, but I swear to you there wasn't a single living soul in the building because they were smart and stayed home where people actually cared about them. I thought I was going to go back early to hang out with my friends but instead I spent the whole week alone. I had never felt so lonely. I felt lonelier now that I had friends and they hated me than when I had moved there and knew not a single living soul.

I went to the movies to see *Her* starring Joaquin Phoenix. The theatre was crammed full, I was alone, and I full out Oprah-ugly-cried. Even though Joaquin's character falls in love with his computer, not a human, I connected with the story on a deep level. I was Joaquin Phoenix—Zach was Scarlet Johansson... That was my story....

They got back on Monday. I was walking to Target. I passed him on the street and he pretended like he didn't know who I was. He didn't look at me, he didn't say anything, he had his headphones in and he just walked by. We lived together. We shared groceries, we shared stories, we shared memories and I could've been—I *was*—some random stranger to him. So I got what I needed at Target, went home and burst through the front door. He was sitting at the table and I said:

"Look! You said everything was going to be the same and you lied! It's not even remotely the same!"

"Well, obviously things are going to be a little different, we're not going to hang out every single day,"

"I'm fine with not hanging out everyday, but we live together and we have memories and we have text messages that show that we were together at some point at least as friends and you can at least have the decency of talking to me when you pass me on the street!

ZACH

"You can at least look me in the eye when I'm talking to you! You can at least pretend for a second that you know who I am! You said everything was going to be the same but you lied, and I should've known from the start, but stupid me worked so hard over Christmas break to get over you—and I think I did pretty well! But listen here; if you think alienating me is going to help this out because you think interacting with me is going to make me fall in love with you again, you're wrong. You're making it worse. You're making me miss you—the you I fell in love with. You're making me fall in love with YOU, YOU before you turned into this asshole you are today. You lied. And just because I used to have feelings for you and just because I might still feel that way a little bit, doesn't mean you have to love me."

8. You Don't Need to Love Me

ZACH
YOU DON'T NEED TO LOVE ME
OR TELL ME THAT YOU DO
DON'T MAKE ME ANY PROMISES,
JUST PROMISE WE'RE NOT THROUGH...
DON'T GIVE ME ONE DAMN THING!
I WON'T LET YOU CALL THIS GREED,
JUST LET ME GIVE TO YOU
THAT'S THE ONLY THING I NEED.
I KNOW THAT THIS CAN WORK
IF YOU PLANT ONE SIMPLE SEED
YOU'D SEE IT GROW...
YOU DON'T NEED TO LOVE ME TO KNOW...

YOU DON'T NEED TO NEED ME.
IT'S BETTER THAT YOU DON'T.
IF EACH OF US CAN WALK AWAY
IT WON'T MATTER THAT I WON'T!
WE'LL BOTH BE SELF-CONTAINED

ZACH

BUT TOGETHER NOT ALONE.
YOU CAN KEEP ME IN THE DARK
HELL, IT'S ALL I'VE EVER KNOWN.
BUT WE BOTH COULD USE A FRIEND
WHO WILL ALWAYS CHECK THE PHONE
AND TAKE THE CALL...
YOU DON'T NEED TO NEED ME AT ALL...

LET ME BE YOUR EMERGENCY CONTACT
YOUR OCCASIONAL PLUS-ONE.
YOUR EXCUSE TO TAKE A SICK-DAY
WHEN THE FORECAST CALLS FOR SUN!
WE CAN KEEP ON BEING LONELY!
BUT WE DON'T HAVE TO BE APART!
AND I'LL NEVER EVEN ASK YOU
TO LET ME HAVE YOUR HEART.
SO I'LL NEVER BREAK YOUR HEART
NO I'LL NEVER BREAK YOUR HEART

YOU DON'T NEED TO LOVE ME
TO LET ME HELP YOU THROUGH.
YOU DON'T NEED TO CONFIDE IN ME,
I'VE GOT CRAP ENOUGH FOR TWO.
YOU DON'T NEED TO ANSWER
I'LL KNOW BEFORE YOU DO.
BUT HEAR ME AND BELIEVE ME
THAT YOU DON'T NEED TO LOVE ME
THE WAY THAT I LOVE YOU...

ZACH

    That was the last time I ever talked to Zach. That was it. The last thing I ever said to Zach was "you lied." And he did... He did lie.

    They started hanging out without me all the time, rubbing it in my face by texting me or sending me Snapchats or posting about it on Twitter.

44

ZACH

They would purposefully go to places where I was just to show that they were fine without me. I was dead inside but they didn't care at all. I hung out with my friend Alison in Oak Park. We were at Five Guys and I sat down and Journey's "Open Arms" came across the radio and I lost it. In the middle of a busy restaurant with people staring at me and Alison shoving napkins in my face begging me to stop—I sobbed. I could not. I couldn't.

I called home every night—more than I ever had in the entire six months that I'd lived there—to say I need someone. I need you. I would call my Grandma and she would answer the phone and I would just sob into the receiver. I called my mom more that week than ever before just to hear a familiar voice. I literally did not talk to anyone while they were across the hall having the time of their lives.

I would sit in our living room and look forward to watching the MSNBC nightly line-up. I looked forward to "spending time with" Rachel Maddow and Chris Matthews. I looked forward to that. Finally, I called my dad one night and told him how sad I was. I didn't know why they were doing this to me and I didn't know how to feel better. He told me now was the time to seriously consider coming home.

I really hadn't even thought about it much, but as soon as he said it I knew it was the right thing to do. It wasn't an easy decision—it was actually the hardest thing I've ever had to do—to drop out of college because my roommate didn't like me. It kills me to say that a boy and some bitch girls forced me out of the place I wanted to be the most.

I started packing up my things. *(he does pack his things)* My room was completely empty and it was all piled up in the living room. On the day my parents came to get me without hesitation, Zach woke up, didn't say a single thing to me, and he walked out the door and he said... Nothing.

I was leaving forever, I was never going to see him again, and he didn't even have the decency to say goodbye, or acknowledge my presence.

ZACH

He didn't look at me, he didn't wave, he said absolutely nothing, he walked out the door, and I never saw him again. As we were loading the car, I kept hoping that every time the doors would open it would be Zach rushing out and begging me to stay. He would tell me it was all a big misunderstanding. But it was always just someone going to class. We drove away and I looked back at the building and thought, "he didn't even let me say goodbye."

Sure, maybe he didn't want to say goodbye to me, but didn't he at least owe me the right to say goodbye to him, to my friends across the hall--to anybody? But he didn't let me.

9. Goodbye My Lover

ZACH

DID I DISAPPOINT YOU? OR LET YOU DOWN?
SHOULD I BE FEELING GUILTY?
OR LET THE JUDGES FROWN?
CAUSE I SAW THE END BEFORE WE'D BEGUN,
YES, I SAW YOU WERE BLINDED
AND I KNEW I HAD WON.
SO I TOOK WHAT'S MINE BY ETERNAL RIGHT.
TOOK YOUR SOUL OUT INTO THE NIGHT.
IT MAY BE OVER, BUT IT WON'T STOP THERE
I AM HERE FOR YOU IF YOU'D ONLY CARE...

YOU TOUCHED MY HEART,
YOU TOUCHED MY SOUL,
CHANGED MY LIFE AND ALL MY GOALS
AND LOVE IS BLIND, BUT THAT I KNEW
WHEN MY HEART WAS BLINDED BY YOU
I'VE KISSED YOUR LIPS AND HELD YOUR HAND
SHARED YOUR DREAMS, SHARED YOUR BED
I KNOW YOU WELL, I KNOW YOUR SMELL
I'VE BEEN ADDICTED TO YOU...

ZACH

GOODBYE, MY LOVER!
GOODBYE, MY FRIEND!
YOU HAVE BEEN THE ONE,
YOU HAVE BEEN THE ONE FOR ME!
GOODBYE, MY LOVER!
GOODBYE, MY FRIEND!
YOU HAVE BEEN THE ONE,
YOU HAVE BEEN THE ONE FOR ME!

I AM A DREAMER AND WHEN I WAKE,
YOU CAN'T BREAK MY SPIRIT!
IT'S MY DREAMS YOU TAKE...
AND AS YOU MOVE ON...
REMEMBER ME... REMEMBER US
AND ALL WE USED TO BE...

I'VE SEEN YOU CRY,
I'VE SEEN YOU SMILE,
I'VE WATCHED YOU SLEEPING FOR A WHILE,
I'D BE THE FATHER OF YOUR CHILD,
I'D SPEND A LIFETIME WITH YOU,
I KNOW YOUR FEARS AND YOU KNOW MINE,
WE'VE HAD OUR DOUBTS,
BUT NOW WE'RE FINE
AND I LOVE YOU, I SWEAR THAT'S TRUE,
I CANNOT LIVE WITHOUT YOU!

GOODBYE, MY LOVER!
GOODBYE, MY FRIEND!
YOU HAVE BEEN THE ONE,
YOU HAVE BEEN THE ONE FOR ME!
GOODBYE, MY LOVER!
GOODBYE, MY FRIEND!
YOU HAVE BEEN THE ONE,
YOU HAVE BEEN THE ONE FOR ME!

ZACH

AND I STILL HOLD YOUR HAND IN MINE...
IN MINE WHEN I'M ASLEEP...
AND I STILL HEAR YOUR VOICE...
SOMETIMES... SAYING "I DON'T LOVE YOU..."

GOODBYE, MY LOVER...
GOODBYE, MY FRIEND...
YOU HAVE BEEN THE ONE...
YOU HAVE BEEN THE ONE FOR ME...
GOODBYE, MY LOVER!
GOODBYE, MY FRIEND!
YOU HAVE BEEN THE ONE!
YOU HAVE BEEN THE ONE FOR ME!

I'M SO HOLLOW, BABY!
I'M SO HOLLOW!
I'M SO, I'M SO, I'M SO HOLLOW!
I'M SO HOLLOW, BABY!
I'M SO HOLLOW!
I'M SO, I'M SO, I' M SO HOLLOW!

ZACH

It's now been over a year since I've spoken to Zach. I'd like to think I've moved on somewhat. I know now how foolish I was. He's not "the one," you're not going to meet "the one," the love-of-your-life at nineteen; we can't all be that lucky. And I know that somewhere down the line there's going to be someone else that I'm going to fall in love with and have children and get married.

I know Zach doesn't ever think about me or miss me, but... I think about him or Chicago or Josey or Jules every single day. Not always in a loving way, some days I think about it and I ask, "why didn't I poop on his pillow?!" and some days I think about it and I say, "why did this happen."

Wherever he is, I wish him nothing but the best.

ZACH

Just because he broke my heart doesn't mean I have to think poorly of him or wish him bad luck or figure out eleven ways to kill him—there are eleven—but I want nothing but the best for him.

I want him to find the person that I fell in love with and bring him back, because he deserves to be that person. Who he is now is not who I fell in love with.

Even though everything is coming up roses for me now, somewhere deep down in the back of my mind, I know that Zach will always be my first love and some parts of me will always love him.

10. It All Fades Away

ZACH

THERE WAS SOMETHING IN A DESERT.
THERE WAS SOME PLACE WILD AND GREEN.
AND A CHILD IN A VILLAGE I PASSED THROUGH.
THERE ARE PLACES THAT I'VE TRAVELLED
AND SO MANY THINGS I'VE SEEN
AND IT ALL FADES AWAY BUT YOU...

I WAS SLIDING DOWN A MOUNTAIN,
I WAS BURNING IN THE SUN,
I WAS CRYING WITH AMAZEMENT AT THE VIEW...
I WAS CAPTURING A MOMENT,
BUT WHEN ALL IS SAID AND DONE, WELL,
IT ALL FADES AWAY BUT YOU...

IT ALL FADES AWAY,
IT ALL FADES AWAY,
IT ALL FADES AWAY BUT YOU...

I HAVE SAILED ACROSS THE OCEANS,
PAST THE CITIES AND THE FARMS,
ON A NEVER ENDING QUEST FOR SOMETHING NEW,

ZACH
AND THE ONLY THING THAT MATTERED
WERE THE FOUR DAYS IN YOUR ARMS
AND IT ALL FADES AWAY BUT YOU...

IT ALL FADES AWAY,
IT ALL FADES AWAY,
IT ALL FADES AWAY BUT YOU...

THERE IS ONE THING THAT'S ETERNAL,
THAT CANNOT BE TORN APART.
THERE IS ONE THIGN THAT REMAINS
FOREVER TRUE...
PAST THE THINKING,
PAST THE BREATHING,
PAST THE BEATING OF MY HEART
IT WILL ALL FADE AWAY BUT YOU!

IT ALL FADES AWAY,
IT ALL FADES AWAY,
IT ALL FADES AWAY BUT YOU!
IT ALL FADES AWAY,
IT ALL FADES AWAY,
IT ALL FADES AWAY...

(ZACH grabs his box and book bag and takes one last look around the dorm room while singing...)

BUT YOU...
BUT YOU...
BUT YOU...
YOU...

(BLACKOUT)

About the Playwright

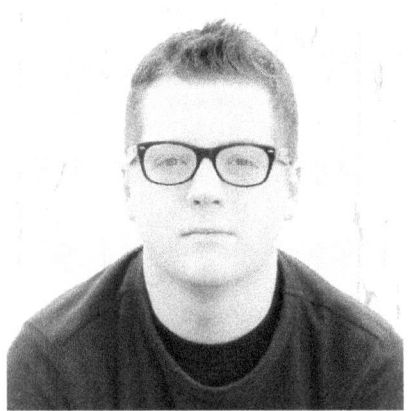

Zach Roberts is a multitalented actor, publisher, producer, playwright, and director with projects on stage, on film and for YouTube, and in print. His work includes the Azooie-Award-winning series *Big Daddy: Ridin' Dirty,* the controversial (and yet-to-be-made) film *Spoiled Breasts,* the upcoming cookbook *This Is What I've Eaten,* and the long-running web vlog *Zach's Vlog.*

Zach's stage career spans nearly a decade of work including originating the role of Pirate Earl in the Dan Hunt musical *The Last Pirates of the Vast Golden Treasure.* He has also portrayed Oswald in *King Lear,* Frederic in *The Pirates of Penzance* and Nathan Detroit in *Guys and Dolls.*

He is the Assistant Director of the Cincinnati acting troupe of the Murder Mystery Company, specializing in murder mystery entertainment. His favorite roles with the company to date include a washed up British rocker turned wedding singer named Dick Johnson and the always-entertaining Detective Peter Ness.

He lives in Springfield, Ohio with his dog, Fran, who was named after Francesca in *The Bridges of Madison County.*

www.ingramcontent.com/pod-product-compliance
Lightning Source LLC
Chambersburg PA
CBHW071004180526
45168CB00003B/1281